What's Awake?

Coyotes

Patricia Whitehouse

Heinemann Library

Chicago, Illinois

© 2003 Reed Educational & Professional Publishing
Published by Heinemann Library,
an imprint of Reed Educational & Professional Publishing,
Chicago, Illinois

Customer Service 888-454-2279
Visit our website at www.heinemannlibrary.com

Designed by Sue Emerson, Heinemann Library
Printed and bound in the United States by Lake Book Manufacturing, Inc.

07
10 9 8 7 6 5 4 3

Library of Congress Cataloging-in-Publication Data
Whitehouse, Patricia, 1958-
    Coyotes / Patricia Whitehouse.
        p. cm. — (What's awake)
Includes index.
Summary: An introduction to the coyote, including its habitat, diet, and physical features.
    ISBN: 978-1-58810-879-1 (1-58810-879-1) (HC), ISBN: 978-1-4034-0626-2 (1-4034-0626-X) (Pbk)
    1. Coyote—Juvenile literature. [1. Coyote.] I. Title.
    QL737.C22 W495 2002
    599.77'25—dc21

                    2001006394

Acknowledgments
The author and publishers are grateful to the following for permission to reproduce copyright material:
p. 4 Steve Strickland/Visuals Unlimited; p. 5 E. R. Degginger/Photo Researchers, Inc.; pp. 6, 14, 16, 20, 22 Jeff Lepore/Photo Researchers, Inc.; p. 7 Tim Davis/Photo Researchers, Inc.; p. 8L Cheryl A. Ertelt/Visuals Unlimited; pp. 8R, 9 Stephen J. Krasemann/Photo Researchers, Inc.; p. 10 Joe McDonald/Visuals Unlimited; p. 11 Andrew Rakoczy/Photo Researchers, Inc.; p. 12 Nicholas DeVore III/Bruce Coleman/PictureQuest; p. 13 Peter Weimann/Animals Animals; p. 15 Victoria Hurst/Tom Stack & Associates; p. 17, 19R Len Rue, Jr./Photo Researchers, Inc.; p. 18 Tom Bledsoe/Photo Researchers, Inc.; p. 19L Paul Berquist/Animals Animals; p. 21 Jerry L. Ferrara/Photo Researchers, Inc.; p. 23 Jack Ballard/Visuals Unlimited.

Cover photograph by Stephen J. Krasemann/Photo Researchers, Inc.

Special thanks to our advisory panel for their help in the preparation of this book:

Eileen Day, Preschool Teacher
Chicago, IL

Ellen Dolmetsch,
Library Media Specialist
Wilmington, DE

Kathleen Gilbert,
Teacher
Round Rock, TX

Sandra Gilbert,
Library Media Specialist
Houston, TX

Angela Leeper,
Educational Consultant
North Carolina Department
of Public Instruction
Raleigh, NC

Pam McDonald, Reading Teacher
Winter Springs, FL

Melinda Murphy,
Library Media Specialist
Houston, TX

The publisher would also like to thank Dr. Dennis Radabaugh, Professor of Zoology at Ohio Wesleyan University in Delaware, Ohio, for his help in reviewing the contents of this book.

Some words are shown in bold, **like this.**
You can find them in the picture glossary on page 23.

Contents

What's Awake?

Some animals are awake when you go to sleep.

Animals that stay awake at night are **nocturnal**.

Coyotes are awake at night.

What Are Coyotes?

Coyotes are **mammals**.

Mammals have **fur**.

Mammals live with their babies.

Mammals make milk for the babies.

What Do Coyotes Look Like?

dog

coyote

Coyotes are the size of German shepherd dogs.

They have yellow-gray **fur**.

Coyotes have thick, bushy tails.

Sometimes coyotes walk with their tails straight out.

Where Do Coyotes Live?

Some coyotes live in deserts.

Some live in mountains or **grasslands**.

Coyotes live where they can find food.

Sometimes they live near people.

What Do Coyotes Do at Night?

Most coyotes wake up just after dark.

They hunt for food.

Most coyotes hunt all night.

Some coyotes only hunt just after dark and before morning.

What Do Coyotes Eat?

In the wild, coyotes usually eat mice, birds, or fish.

They might eat bugs or fruit.

In the city, coyotes eat these things, too.

They also eat garbage or food people leave out for their pets.

What Do Coyotes Sound Like?

Coyotes can yelp and growl.

They can bark, too.

muzzle

Coyotes can howl.

They hold their **muzzles** straight up to the sky.

How Are Coyotes Special?

Coyotes have a good sense of smell.

They can smell food from far away.

Coyotes can live in different places.

They live where it is hot and where it is cold.

Where Do Coyotes Go during the Day?

In the morning, coyotes find a safe spot.

Then they curl up and sleep.

Sometimes coyotes hunt during the day.

They do this if they can't find food at night.

Coyote Map

fur

muzzle

tail

Picture Glossary

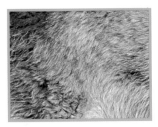
fur
pages 6, 8

muzzle
page 17

grasslands
page 10

nocturnal
page 4

mammal
pages 6, 7

Note to Parents and Teachers

Reading for information is an important part of a child's literacy development. Learning begins with a question about something. Help children think of themselves as investigators and researchers by encouraging their questions about the world around them. In this book, the animal is identified as a mammal. A mammal by definition is one that is covered with hair or fur and that feeds its young with milk from its body. The symbol for mammal in the picture glossary is of a dog nursing its babies. Point out the fact that, although the photograph for mammal shows a dog, many other animals are mammals—including humans.

! **CAUTION:** Remind children that it is not a good idea to handle wild animals. Children should wash their hands with soap and water after they touch any animal.

Index